Celebrating New Year

Carmel Reilly

Australia • Brazil • Japan • Korea • Mexico • Singapore • Spain • United Kingdom • United States

Celebrating New Year

Fast Forward
Yellow Level 6

Text: Carmel Reilly
Illustrations: Margaret Krajnc
Editor: Kate McGough
Series design: James Lowe
Design: Vonda Pestana
Production controller: Hanako Smith
Photo Research: Gillian Cardinal
Audio recordings: Juliet Hill, Picture Start
Spoken by: Matthew King and Abbe Holmes

Acknowledgements
The author and publisher would like to acknowledge permission to reproduce material from the following sources: Photographs by AAP Image/Anupam Nath, pp 3, 4 top/Bernd Settnik, p9/Roy Pohan, pp 10-11/Valdrin Xhemaj, p4 bottom; APL/Corbis/Keren Su, cover, p1; Getty Images/Samba Photo, p5 bottom/The Image Bank/Hiroyuki, p6; Liquid Library, p12; Lonely Planet Images/Alain Evrard, p5 top/Greg Elms, p14/Gary Weare, pp 14-15; PhotoEdit/Michael Newman, p13; photolibrary.com/Graham Monro, p7; Robert Harding Images, p15.

ISBN 978 0 17 012496 6
ISBN 978 0 17 012489 8 (set)

Cengage Learning Australia
Level 7, 80 Dorcas Street
South Melbourne, Victoria Australia 3205
Phone: 1300 790 853

Cengage Learning New Zealand
Unit 4B Rosedale Office Park
331 Rosedale Road, Albany, North Shore NZ 0632
Phone: 0508 635 766

For learning solutions, visit cengage.com.au

Printed in Australia by Ligare Pty Ltd
8 9 10 11 12 13 14 20 19 18 17 16

THE UNIVERSITY OF MELBOURNE

Evaluated in independent research by staff from the Department of Language, Literacy and Arts Education at the University of Melbourne.

Celebrating New Year

Carmel Reilly

Contents

Chapter 1

CELEBRATING NEW YEAR

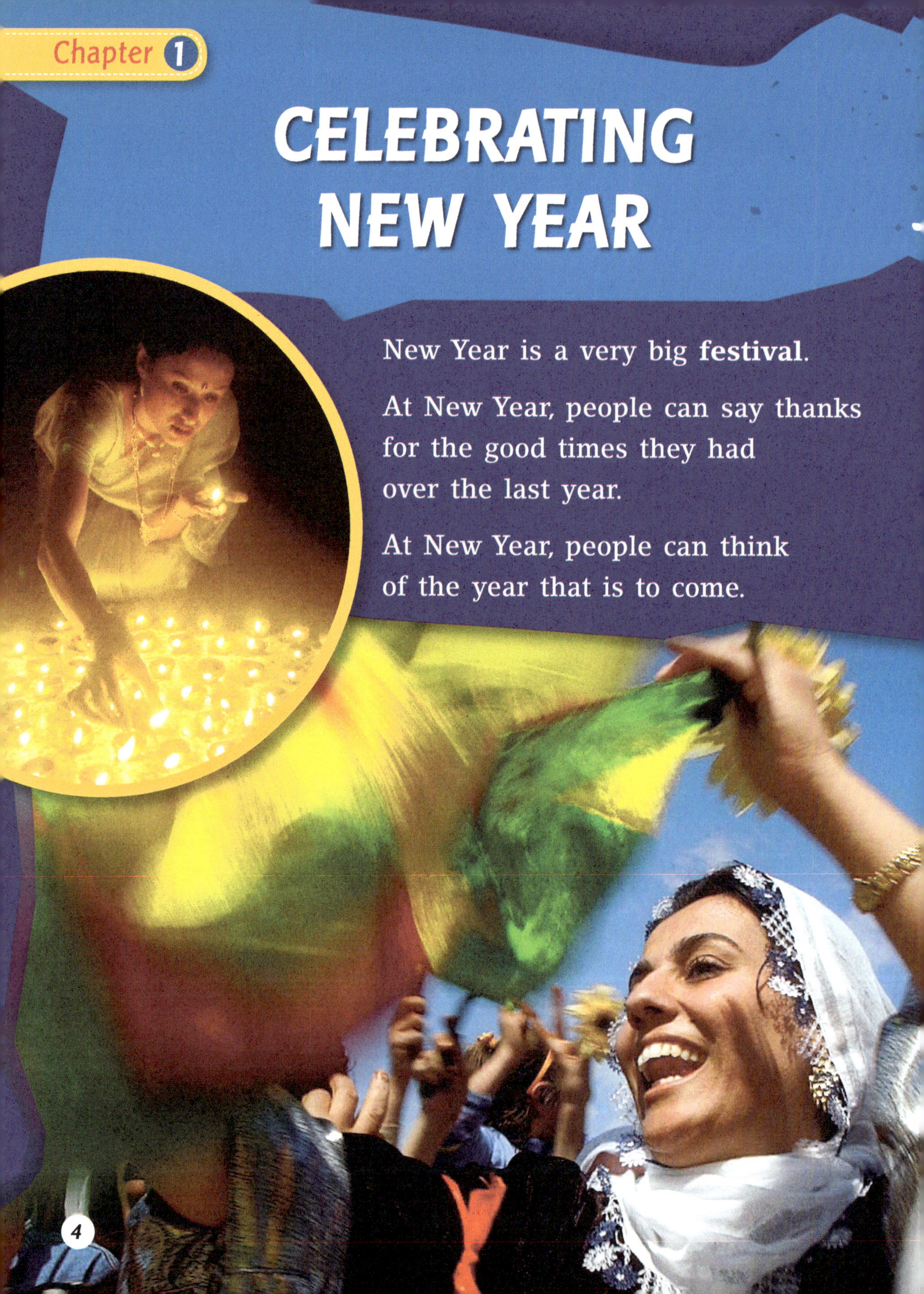

New Year is a very big **festival**.

At New Year, people can say thanks for the good times they had over the last year.

At New Year, people can think of the year that is to come.

New Year is the time
to say goodbye
to the old year.
New Year is the time
to celebrate the coming
of the new year.

New Year is **celebrated** by people all over the world.

A lot of people have come here to celebrate the coming of New Year.

People celebrate New Year
in a lot of ways.

But not all people celebrate New Year
at the one time.

New Year is an old festival.

In very old times, a lot of people celebrated the New Year with the coming of spring.

Other people celebrated the New Year in the autumn.

Today, a lot of people celebrate New Year on 1 January.

But, as we will see, in a lot of places people celebrate New Year at other times.

Running Words 126

Fact Box

The first place to celebrate New Year's Day is Kiribati.

The last place to celebrate New Year's Day is Samoa.

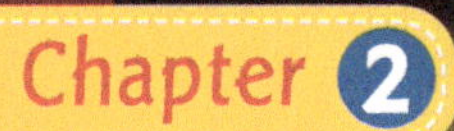

CHINESE NEW YEAR

Chinese New Year is celebrated in January in some years, and in February in other years. It is a big festival for Chinese people, and it goes on for three days and three nights.

Chinese people like to go out and have a good time as they celebrate the coming of the New Year.

Chapter 3

JEWISH NEW YEAR

Jewish New Year is in autumn.
It is celebrated over two days.
It is the time when Jewish people look back over the old year.
It is also the time when they think of the year to come.

Jewish people like to stay at home at New Year. They make and eat a lot of special food.

INDIAN NEW YEAR

In India, New Year is celebrated in a lot of ways and with a lot of special foods.

In some places in India, there are festivals in spring.

In other places,
there is one big festival in autumn
that goes on for five days
and five nights.

Glossary

autumn the season between summer and winter

celebrated took part in and had fun at a special event

festival a special event, often held at the same time each year

Index